CAUSE AND EFFECT

Expanding a NATION

CAUSES AND EFFECTS

of the Louisiana Purchase

BY ELIZABETH RAUM

Consultant:
Malcolm J. Rohrbough
Professor Emeritus
Department of History
The University of Iowa

CAPSTONE PRESS
a capstone imprint

Fact Finders Books are published by Capstone Press,
1710 Roe Crest Drive, North Mankato, Minnesota 56003
www.capstonepub.com

Library of Congress Cataloging-in-Publication Data
Raum, Elizabeth.
Expanding a nation : causes and effects of the Louisiana Purchase / by Elizabeth Raum.
pages cm.—(Fact finders. Cause and effect)
Includes bibliographical references and index.
Summary: "Describes the causes of and effects of the Louisiana Purchase on U.S.
history"—Provided by publisher.
ISBN 978-1-4765-0236-6 (library binding)—ISBN 978-1-4765-3402-2 (pbk.)—
ISBN 978-1-4765-3410-7 (ebook pdf)
1. Louisiana Purchase—Juvenile literature. 2. United States—Territorial expansion—
Juvenile literature. 3. United States—History—1801-1809—Juvenile literature. I. Title.
E333.R38 2014
973.4'6—dc23   2013007025

Editorial Credits
Erika L. Shores, editor; Alison Thiele, designer; Svetlana Zhurkin, media researcher;
Laura Manthe, production specialist

Photo Credits
Bridgeman Art Library: Peter Newark American Pictures/Private Collection, 19; Corbis:
Bettmann, cover (middle), 10, 14, 17, 21; Courtesy Scotts Bluff National Monument,
20; iStockphotos: Steven Wynn, 13; Library of Congress, cover (inset), 8, 9, 28, 29;
Newscom: Album/Oronoz, 11, Everett Collection, 16, Picture History, 25; North Wind
Picture Archives, 4, 7, 26

Printed in the United States of America in Brainerd, Minnesota.
032013   007721BANGF13

Table OF CONTENTS

A Big PURCHASE

In 1803 the United States was still a small, young country. Just 17 states made up the Union, stretching from the Atlantic coast to the Mississippi River. European countries claimed the rest of the land in North America.

New Orleans, Louisiana, was founded in 1718. It was a center for trade, and a big reason for the Louisiana Purchase.

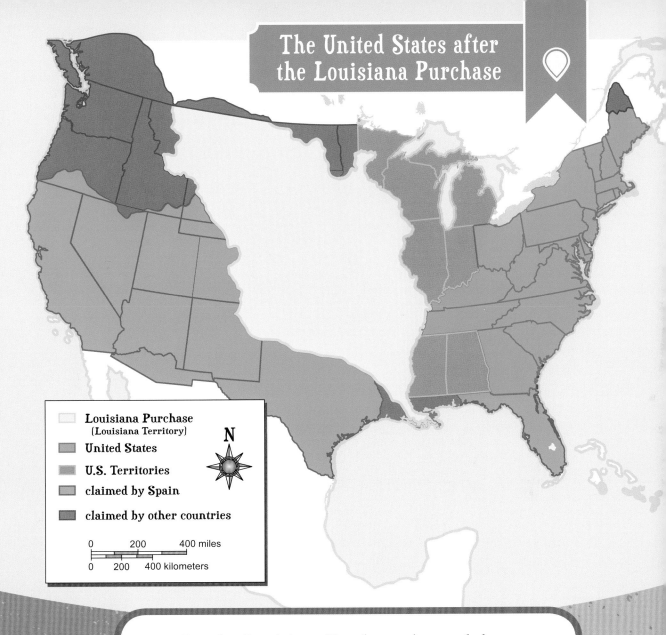

Louisiana Purchase
(Louisiana Territory)

United States

U.S. Territories

claimed by Spain

claimed by other countries

N

0   200   400 miles

0   200   400 kilometers

But the Louisiana Purchase changed that. The United States bought a huge area of land from France. The new land doubled the size of the country overnight. The Louisiana Purchase was an event that changed the future of the nation.

What Caused the LOUISIANA PURCHASE?

Buying the Louisiana Territory was a big move by the United States. And it all started with a need for a river.

Cause #1—United States' Need for a River Route

The mighty Mississippi River flows south from what is now Minnesota to the Gulf of Mexico. Americans needed a good river route to ship goods. The Mississippi was perfect for the job. But there was only one problem. The United States didn't actually own the river.

France first claimed the Mississippi River Valley in 1682. The area was named Louisiana, in honor of King Louis XIV. In 1762 France made a deal with Spain. Spain took control of Louisiana and the Mississippi.

port: a harbor or place where boats and ships can dock or anchor safely

Traders used large flatboats to move cargo up and down the Mississippi River.

After the Revolutionary War (1775–1783), Americans began moving west. Spanish officials worried that American settlers would try to take over Spanish-owned land and the important **port** city of New Orleans. In 1784 they stopped allowing goods to be shipped on the Mississippi. They reversed their decision in 1795 but stopped river trade again three years later. American leaders knew they needed to get control of the river if the United States was going to become a world power.

Cause #2—France Makes a Move

France's leader, Napoleon Bonaparte, wanted to build an **empire** in Europe and North America. In October 1800 he made a secret deal with Spain to take back New Orleans and Louisiana. Napoleon hoped secrecy would give him time to send French troops to protect Louisiana.

In 1801 President Thomas Jefferson learned that France had reclaimed Louisiana. Jefferson was horrified. He thought France had grown too powerful. He didn't want France to control American trade routes. Jefferson said that France owning Louisiana was the greatest threat to the United States since the Revolutionary War. He began thinking about trying to buy Louisiana from France.

President Thomas Jefferson feared France would take control of trade routes in the United States.

empire: a large territory ruled by a powerful leader

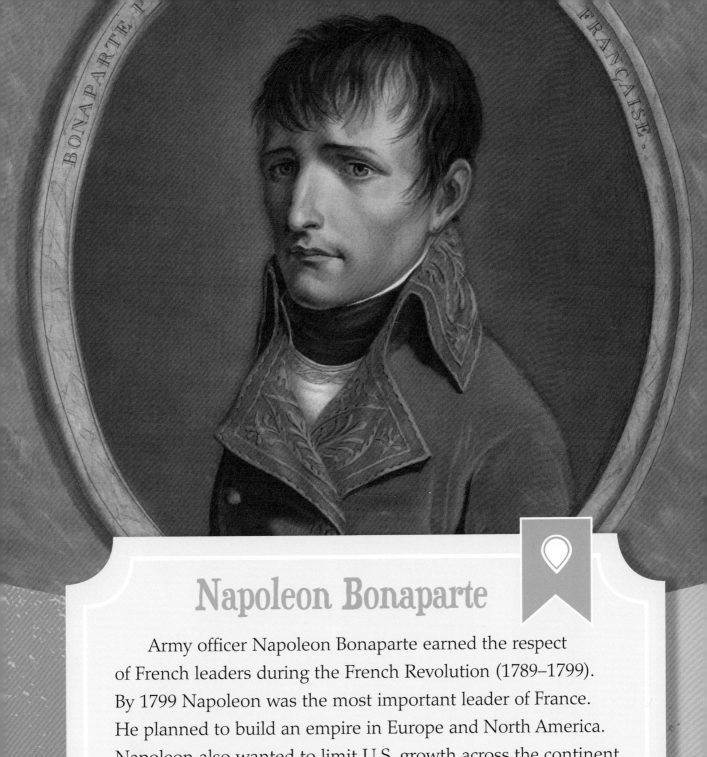

Napoleon Bonaparte

Army officer Napoleon Bonaparte earned the respect of French leaders during the French Revolution (1789–1799). By 1799 Napoleon was the most important leader of France. He planned to build an empire in Europe and North America. Napoleon also wanted to limit U.S. growth across the continent. For his plan to succeed, he needed control of Louisiana.

Cause #3—Napoleon's Fading Dream

Part of Napoleon's reason for wanting Louisiana was its location. France owned the island of Saint-Domingue in the Caribbean Sea. Valuable crops such as sugar and coffee were raised there. France could use the port of New Orleans to ship these crops to Europe.

But by 1802 Napoleon's dreams of a North American empire were beginning to fade. French troops lost to rebelling slaves in Saint-Domingue. Napoleon no longer needed Louisiana to support Saint-Domingue.

FAST FACT: Today Saint-Domingue is called Haiti.

Rebelling slaves in Saint-Domingue defeated the French army.

Cause #4—Napoleon's Need for Cash

France and Great Britain had been in conflict over land in North America since the mid-1700s. But after the loss of Saint-Domingue, Napoleon no longer wanted to fight Britain in North America. By 1803 Napoleon knew that if he kept Louisiana, the British might invade from Canada. He would rather invade Britain from France. If he sold Louisiana, he would have the money to finance that attack. Napoleon sent his advisors to meet with Jefferson's advisors. Could they make a deal?

Buying LOUISIANA

In 1801 Jefferson appointed Robert Livingston the U.S. minister to France. Jefferson ordered Livingston to buy land on the lower Mississippi, including New Orleans.

Jefferson convinced Congress to authorize $2 million to buy the land. If France refused, Jefferson threatened to help the British. Napoleon didn't want American forces working with the British in a war against France.

For two years Livingston tried to get France to accept the deal. But Napoleon's representatives wouldn't agree. In January 1803 Jefferson sent James Monroe to France to help Livingston. Monroe was the minister to Great Britain. Jefferson also sweetened the deal. He told Monroe to pay as much as $10 million to buy New Orleans.

FAST FACT: James Monroe was a close friend of Thomas Jefferson. Monroe also owned land in the West. He would benefit from the Louisiana Territory being under U.S. control. Jefferson knew Monroe would work hard to make a deal with France.

James Monroe would become U.S. president 14 years after the Louisiana Purchase.

On April 30, 1803, Monroe and Livingston reached a deal with Napoleon's advisors.

Taking a Chance

For four days Livingston and Monroe **negotiated** with Napoleon's advisors. The French wanted $15 million. That was $5 million more than Jefferson had approved. But the larger sum included more land than the United States was requesting. France was offering the entire Louisiana Territory, which was 529,402,880 acres (214,241,744 hectares).

There was no way to get permission from Jefferson. There were no telephones or e-mail in 1803. Letters traveled by ship, which meant a two-month delay. Livingston and Monroe decided to go ahead with the deal. They hoped Jefferson and Congress would agree.

Jefferson learned about the purchase on June 30, 1803. He was pleased, even though it cost more than he had authorized. The cost ended up being about 3 cents an acre—a bargain even in those days.

But Jefferson worried that the Louisiana Purchase was illegal. There was nothing in the U.S. Constitution about purchasing new lands. He thought the country might need to **amend** the Constitution to allow the purchase.

negotiate: to arrange a deal
amend: to change

But Jefferson couldn't worry for long. Livingston sent word that Napoleon was becoming impatient about the delay in completing the sale. Livingston thought Napoleon might change his mind. Jefferson sprang into action. The deal wouldn't go into effect until the Senate approved it. Jefferson asked the Senate to **ratify** the Louisiana Purchase Treaty. It did so by a vote of 24 to 7 on October 20, 1803.

Congress approved the purchase, but it didn't have the money to pay for it. The government borrowed the money from banks in Europe. It had 15 years to repay the loan.

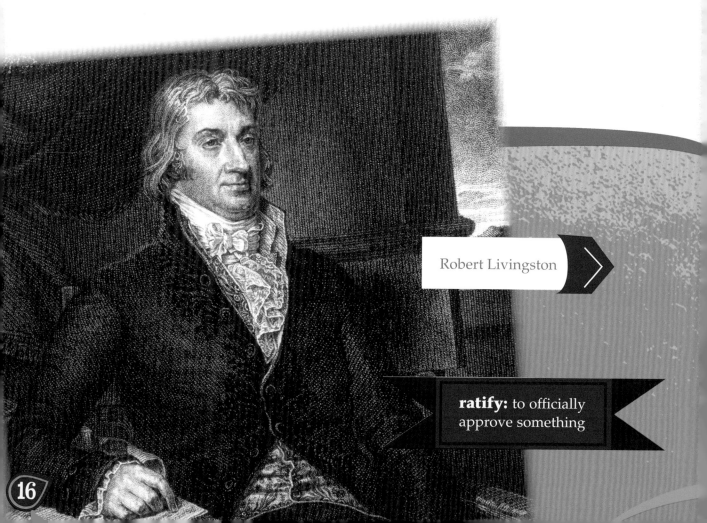

Robert Livingston >

ratify: to officially approve something

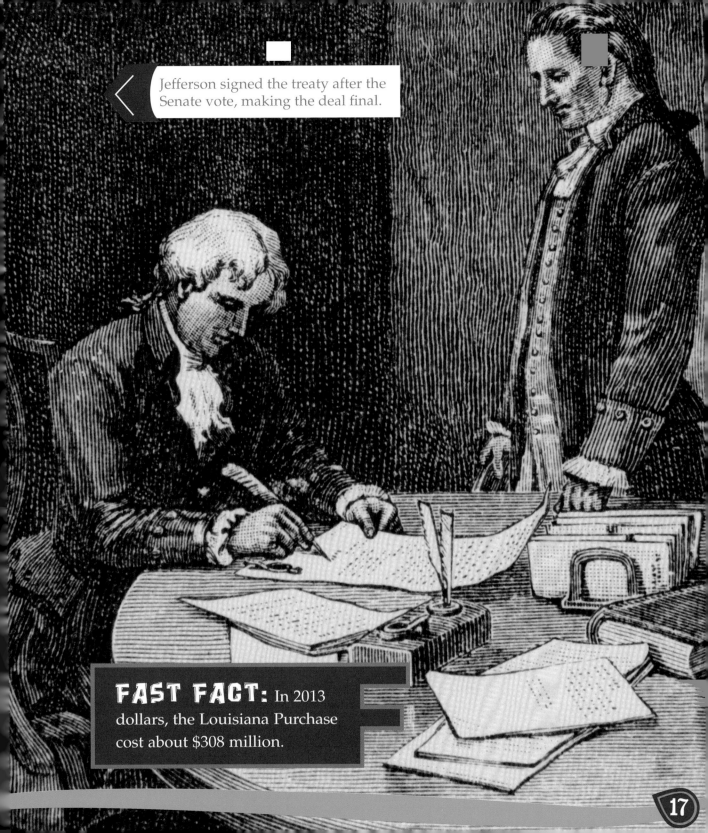

Jefferson signed the treaty after the Senate vote, making the deal final.

FAST FACT: In 2013 dollars, the Louisiana Purchase cost about $308 million.

What Effects Did THE LOUISIANA PURCHASE HAVE?

No one knew the exact boundaries of the Louisiana Territory. The Mississippi River formed the eastern boundary. The Rocky Mountains marked the western border. The northern boundary wasn't established until 1818 when the United States and Great Britain agreed to the current Canadian border.

Jefferson thought the territory's southern boundary was the Rio Grande River. That meant that much of present-day Texas was included. Spain, which claimed Texas at the time, disagreed. In 1806 the two countries worked out a **compromise**. By 1821 they agreed to use the Sabine River as the boundary between Texas and Louisiana.

The Louisiana Purchase changed the United States and the lives of its people forever. Some of these effects are still felt today.

compromise: a settlement in which each side gives up part of its demands

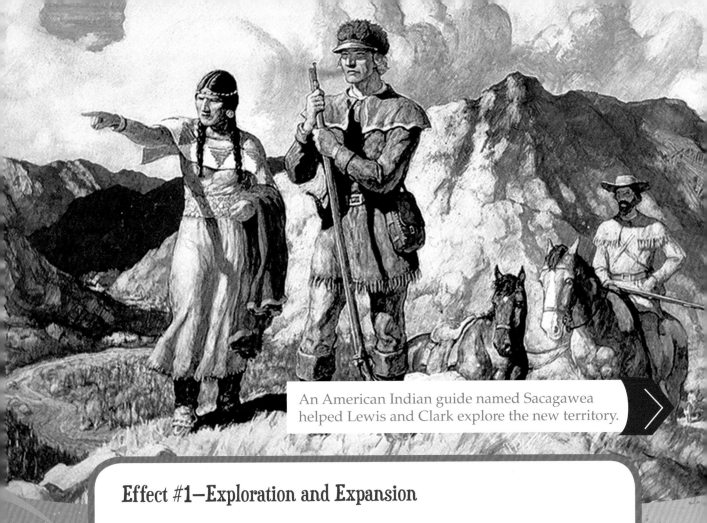

An American Indian guide named Sacagawea helped Lewis and Clark explore the new territory.

Effect #1—Exploration and Expansion

The Louisiana Purchase spurred a great westward movement. In 1803 Jefferson sent Meriwether Lewis, William Clark, and their team to explore the new land.

The journey took more than two years. Lewis and Clark mapped the rivers and mountains. They kept journals and described unfamiliar plants and animals. They wrote about American Indians, including their languages and customs. Their journals gave Americans the first glimpse of the American West. Soon other explorers were making trails west.

As people moved west, they started farms and ranches in the rich soil of the Louisiana Territory. The area earned the nickname "America's breadbasket."

In 1841 the first settlers traveled the Oregon Trail to California and Oregon. Between 1840 and 1870 about 500,000 settlers traveled on the trail.

In 1848 James Marshall discovered gold in California. The discovery meant the trickle of settlers going west became a flood. Gold wasn't the only natural resource of the West. Silver, oil, coal, and iron ore helped to turn the United States into a rich and powerful nation.

The Oregon Trail led settlers to a new life in the West.

Miners set up camps along streams to look for gold.

Exploring the Louisiana Territory

Date	Explorers	Area
1804–1806	Lewis and Clark Expedition	explored from St. Louis northwest to the Pacific coast
1804–1805	Dunbar-Hunter Expedition	explored Arkansas and Louisiana
1806	Freeman and Custis Expedition	explored from the Red River through Arkansas to Texas
1806–1807	Zebulon Pike Expedition	explored the Rocky Mountains

Montana

North Dakota

Minnesota

South Dakota

Wyoming

Nebraska

Iowa

Colorado

Kansas

Missouri

New Mexico

Oklahoma

Arkansas

Texas

Louisiana

Effect #2—A Larger, Stronger Nation

The Louisiana Purchase doubled the size of the United States. People wondered if such a large country could survive. Jefferson believed it could.

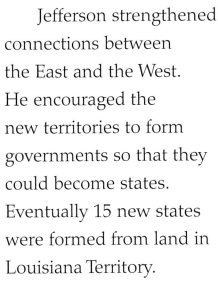

Jefferson strengthened connections between the East and the West. He encouraged the new territories to form governments so that they could become states. Eventually 15 new states were formed from land in Louisiana Territory.

The Louisiana Purchase increased the power of the **federal** government to add territory and borrow money. The nation became stronger as a result.

federal: central or national

Joining the Union

State*	Date Admitted to the United States
Louisiana	1812
Missouri*	1821
Arkansas*	1836
Texas	1845
Iowa*	1846
Minnesota	1858
Kansas*	1861
Nebraska*	1867
Colorado	1876
North Dakota	1889
South Dakota	1889
Montana	1889
Wyoming	1890
Oklahoma*	1907
New Mexico	1912

*States marked with an asterisk are completely within the boundaries of the Louisiana Purchase.

Effect #3—A Changed Way of Life

White settlers believed they had a right to move onto all western lands. The surge of settlers had a terrible effect on American Indians who lived west of the Mississippi. Settlers killed the buffalo that many Indians depended on to survive. Many native people died of diseases such as smallpox brought by the settlers. Others were killed in battles with settlers or the army.

The American Indians that survived were forced to leave the lands they had lived on for generations. By 1890 nearly all American Indian groups had been forced to move to **reservations**. Most reservations were located on poor land with few natural resources. Most Indian children had to go to boarding schools. They weren't allowed to speak their native languages or practice their cultural traditions.

reservation: an area of land set aside by the government for American Indians

The U.S. government forced American Indians on long journeys to reservations in the West.

Slaves harvested sugarcane on Southern plantations.

Effect #4—Dealing with Slavery

The Louisiana Purchase forced the United States to address the issue of slavery. By 1800 Northern states and territories had **abolished** slavery. But slavery was allowed in Southern states. Southern farmers insisted they needed African-American slave labor to run their large plantations.

When the United States bought Louisiana, government leaders had to decide if slavery would be allowed to spread west. Many Northerners wanted to ban slavery in the Louisiana Territory. Southerners disagreed.

Debate over slavery in the new states and territories continued for the next 40 years. By 1861 the debate was so heated that 11 Southern states left the Union to form the Confederate States of America. This action sparked the Civil War (1861–1865). When the Union won the war, slavery was outlawed throughout the United States.

abolish: to officially put an end to something

Cause and Effect—A Changed Nation

The Louisiana Purchase greatly expanded the size of the United States. The country became far bigger than any European country. The vast resources in the Louisiana Territory helped the United States develop major industries. The nation's size, population, and natural resources helped make it a world power.

Railways built through the Louisiana Territory allowed people and goods to travel across the United States.

European immigrants settled in areas that became new states, such as Nebraska. Homes there were made of sod and grass because wood was scarce.

American Indians, African slaves, and French and Spanish people made their homes in the Louisiana Territory. After the Louisiana Purchase, immigrants from Northern Europe and Russia moved there. So did settlers from the eastern United States. Over time these people learned to live together, despite their differences. This diverse population changed the face of America. The nation had to rethink what it meant to be an American.

GLOSSARY

abolish (uh-BAH-lish)—to officially put an end to something

amend (uh-MEND)—to change

compromise (KAHM-pruh-myz)—a settlement in which each side gives up part of its demands

empire (EM-pire)—a large territory ruled by a powerful leader

expedition (ek-spuh-DI-shuhn)—a long journey for a certain purpose

federal (FED-ur-uhl)—central or national

minister (MIN-uh-stur)—a high-ranking government official who advises the leader

negotiate (ni-GOH-shee-ate)—to bargain or discuss something to come to an agreement

port (PORT)—a harbor or place where boats and ships can dock or anchor safely

ratify (RA-ti-fye)—to officially approve something

reservation (rez-er-VAY-shuhn)—an area of land set aside by the U.S. government for American Indians

territory (TERR-uh-tor-ee)—an area of land that is not yet a state

READ MORE

Fradin, Dennis B. *The Louisiana Purchase.* Turning Points in U.S. History. Tarrytown, N.Y.: Marshall Cavendish Benchmark, 2010.

Roza, Greg. *Westward Expansion.* The Story of America. New York: Gareth Stevens Pub., 2011.

Sharp, Constance. *Thomas Jefferson and the Growing United States (1800-1811).* How America Became America. Philadelphia: Mason Crest Publishers, 2012.

Shea, Therese. *The Louisiana Purchase.* New York: PowerKids Press, 2009.

INTERNET SITES

FactHound offers a safe, fun way to find Internet sites related to this book. All of the sites on FactHound have been researched by our staff.

Here's all you do:

Visit *www.facthound.com*

Type in this code: 9781476502366

Check out projects, games and lots more at
www.capstonekids.com

CRITICAL THINKING USING THE
COMMON CORE

1. Suppose that the United States had not been able to buy the Louisiana Territory. How do you think the development of the United States might have changed? (Integration of Knowledge and Ideas)

2. Describe the effect of the Louisiana Purchase on American Indians in the years following the purchase. Use details from the text to support your answer. (Key Ideas and Details)

3. Examine the chart on page 23. What does this chart tell you about the long-term effects of the Louisiana Purchase? How did the Louisiana Purchase strengthen the United States? (Craft and Structure)

INDEX